MEMBER OF PARLIAMENT

Rebecca Hunter

**Photography by
Chris Fairclough**

CHERRYTREE BOOKS

A Cherrytree book

First published in 2009 by
Evans Brothers Ltd
2A Portman Mansions
Chiltern Street
London W1U 6NR

British Library Cataloguing in Publication Data
Hunter, Rebecca, 1935-
    Member of Parliament - (People who help us)
    1. Legislators - Great Britain - Juvenile literature
    2. Great Britain - Politics and government - Juvenile literature
    I. Title
    328.3'3'0941

ISBN-13: 9781842345467

Planned and produced by Discovery Books Ltd
Editor: Rebecca Hunter
Designer: Ian Winton

Acknowledgements
Commissioned photography by Chris Fairclough.
Additional photography: Photolibrary/Robert Harding Travel/Adam Woolfit p16.

The author, packager and publisher would like to thank Edward and Emily Davey, Ceri Finnegan and the
Staff of the Houses of Parliament for their help and participation in this book.

Words appearing in bold, **like this**, are explained in the glossary.

Contents

I am an MP

My name is Edward. I am an MP or Member of Parliament. I work at the **Houses of Parliament** in London.

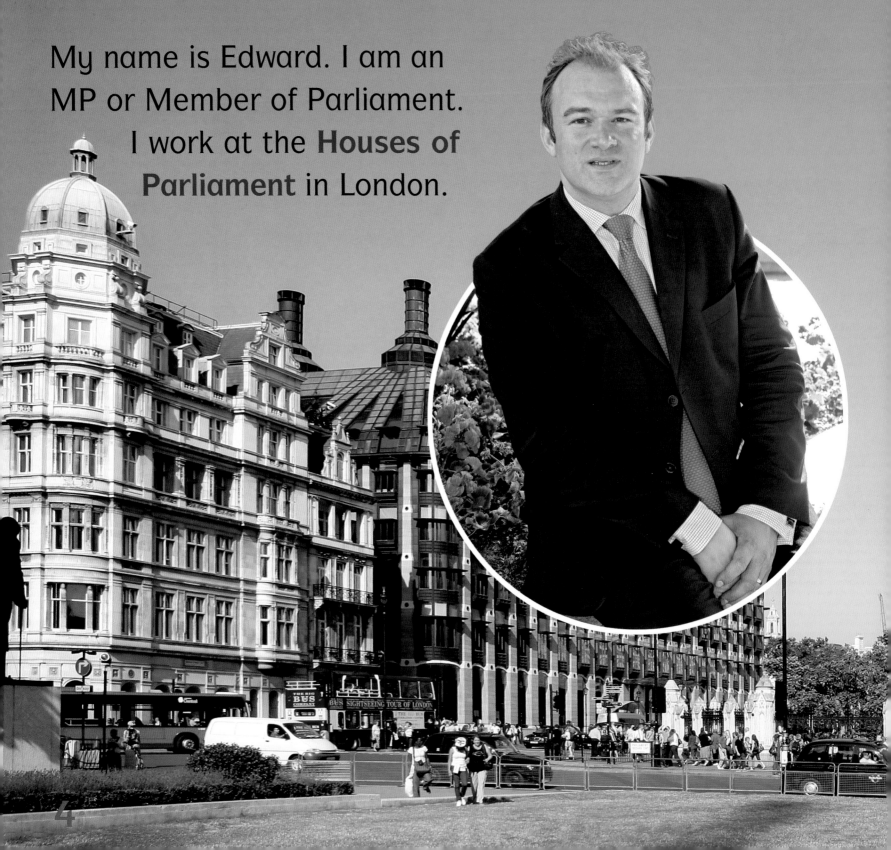

This is the place where we discuss new laws that the **government** wants to make. The government is in charge of the country. Its leader is the Prime Minister.

My family

I live with my family in my **consitituency**, Kingston in south London.

This is my wife Emily, and our baby boy, John.

After breakfast I say
goodbye to Emily and
John and leave the house.

I am going to my
constituency office.

In my office

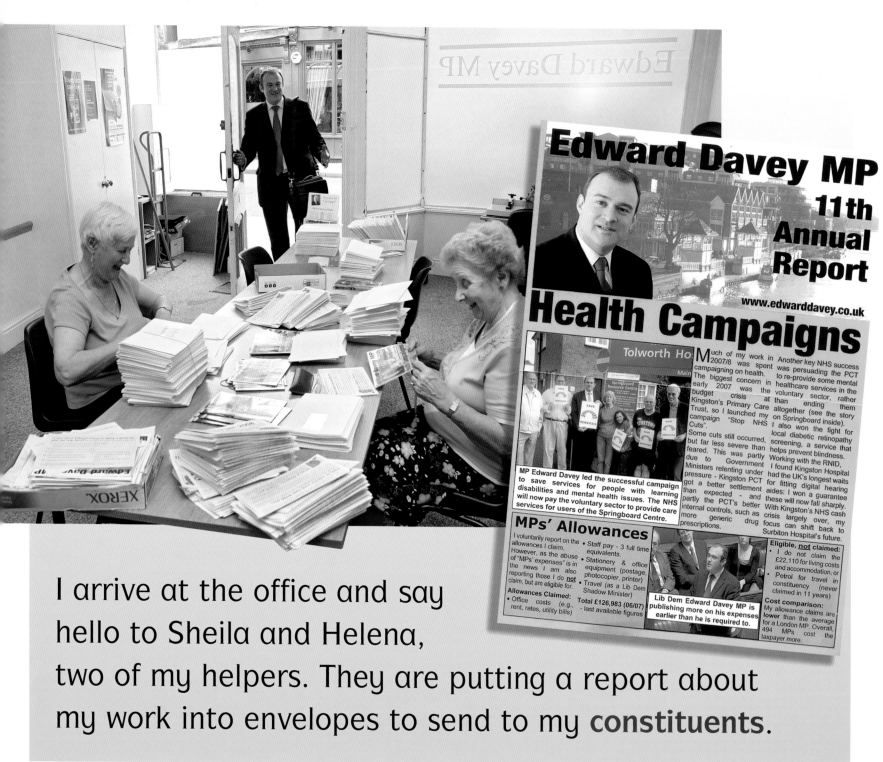

I arrive at the office and say
hello to Sheila and Helena,
two of my helpers. They are putting a report about
my work into envelopes to send to my **constituents**.

This is Mr Parekh, one of my constituents. I am trying to help him with his housing problems.

Later I write some letters to **government ministers**. I am asking them to help me assist other people in my community.

School visit

Today I am visiting a local infants' school. I meet the head teacher and some of the children in the playground. The children lead me along the number snake to their new notice board.

This information board was put up so that everyone could find out what was happening in the school each week.

In the classroom I talk to the children. They tell me about their favourite lessons. Then they ask me what it is like being an MP.

In the book corner, they choose a book for me to read to them.

Going to London

Next I get on the train to go to central London. I do some work on my laptop. It is easy to write letters and read **documents** on the train.

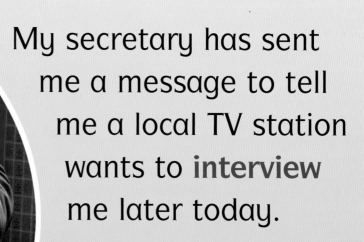

My secretary has sent me a message to tell me a local TV station wants to **interview** me later today.

It is a lovely sunny day in London. The streets are full of tourists on holiday. I enjoy the walk to my London office.

My London office

At the entrance to my London office building is an armed security guard. He asks to see my **security pass** before he will let me in.

This is Ceri, my secretary. She gives me some letters to sign and tells me about my **appointments** today.

I have a quick cup of coffee and read my mail.

The Houses of Parliament

This is the Chamber of the House of Commons, part of the Houses of Parliament. It is where MPs meet and have **debates** with each other about new laws and **policies**.

Most MPs belong to one of the three main **political parties** - Labour, Conservative or Liberal Democrat. I am a Liberal Democrat MP.

There are no debates today, but I have a meeting in the Houses of Parliament with some other Liberal Democrat MPs. We are discussing our ideas for protecting the environment and stopping climate change.

After our meeting I just have time to get a quick lunch from the cafeteria.

Petition to No. 10

This afternoon I have to take a **petition** to No.10 Downing Street. This is where the Prime Minister lives.

We are **campaigning** for cheaper train fares from my constituency. More than 500 people have signed this petition.

The armed police guard unlocks the gate and lets me through.

18

I knock on the door of No.10.

One of the **staff** comes to the door. He takes the petition. I hope the Prime Minister will agree with our petition and help get the fares reduced.

Tea on the terrace

I have invited some of my constituents to tea. This family have a son, Toby, who wants to be an MP. He wrote and asked if I would meet him.

We take our tea out on to the terrace next to the River Thames.

Toby asks about being an MP. He wants to know what subjects he should study. He says he enjoys taking part in debates at school. I think he would make a good MP.

Giving an interview

Before I go home, a local TV news station interviews me about a campaign to improve the **health service** in my area. The interview will be shown on television later this week.

It has been a busy day, but I love being an MP. It is a rewarding job because you can help people in many different ways.

Glossary

appointment an arranged time for a meeting with someone

campaigning working in an organized way towards a particular goal

constituency the area in which the people who have elected an MP live

constituents the people who live in an MP's constituency

debates discussions about important things by two or more groups of people

documents papers containing information

government the organization that is in charge of the country. The government proposes new laws, raises taxes and spends money on things like schools, roads and the army.

government ministers the most important people in the government, chosen by the Prime Minister

health service the organization that cares for our health

Houses of Parliament the place where MPs meet. It is divided into the House of Commons and the House of Lords.

interview a conversation with a journalist or television presenter

petition a document asking for action that has been signed by a lot of people

policies ideas or actions suggested by groups of people

political parties groups of people with different ideas of how to run the country

security pass a special card allowing you to enter a building

staff the people who work for an organization

Index